WAY OF THE ASCETICS

WAY OF THE ASCETICS

Tito Colliander

Translated by Katharine Ferré
Introduction by Kenneth Leech

1817

Harper & Row, Publishers, San Francisco

Cambridge, Hagerstown, New York, Philadelphia
London, Mexico City, São Paulo, Sydney

WAY OF THE ASCETICS. Copyright © 1960 by Tito Colliander. Introduction copyright © 1982 by Kenneth
Leech. All rights reserved. Printed in the United States
of America. No part of this book may be used or repro-
duced in any manner whatsoever without written per-
mission except in the case of brief quotations embodied
in critical articles and reviews. For information address
Harper & Row, Publishers, Inc., 10 East 53rd Street,
New York, NY 10022. Published simultaneously in
Canada by Fitzhenry & Whiteside, Limited, Toronto.
Translated from the Swedish, *Asketernas Väg,* which
was first published in 1952 by Söderström & Co., Hel-
singfors, Finland.

Designer: Jim Mennick

Library of Congress Cataloging in Publication Data

Colliander, Tito, 1904–
WAY OF THE ASCETICS.

Translation of: Asketernas väg.
Includes index.
1. Asceticism—Orthodox Eastern Church. I. Title.
BV5035.C6413 1982   248.4'7   81-13171
ISBN 0-06-061526-5   AACR2

82 83 84 85 86 10 9 8 7 6 5 4 3 2 1

CONTENTS

INTRODUCTION

IN the last two decades, both the degree of secularization and the extent of the resurgence of interest in spirituality have been grossly exaggerated. To some extent, the exaggeration of the former led to that of the latter: so one saw the remarkable *volte-face* of those who in the 1960s had hailed the "secular city" and the "death of God" appearing equally uncritically as protagonists of Eastern mysticism in the seventies. Of course, our society never became totally secular, totally irreligious, and the current spiritual revival has not affected all groups of society to the same extent. Much of our culture remains consistently conventional, as much in its religion as in its general attitudes. And nothing is more opposed to true spirituality than conventional religion. From such religion, atheism is a liberating experience.

Nevertheless, the rejection of conventional religion has led many to explore more deeply the resources of Christian traditions other than and deeper than their own. Although we have heard a good deal about the popularity of non-Christian spiritual disciplines from the East, an equally striking phenomenon has been the rediscovery of the Eastern Christian traditions. In the United States today, the Orthodox churches are an integral part of the religious scene. Yet many Western Christians are only beginning to become familiar with the riches of Orthodoxy—its theology, its liturgical life, its concern with the inner life of prayer that can do so much to enrich and deepen our often superficial religious life.

It is with the spiritual tradition of Eastern Orthodoxy that Tito Colliander is concerned in this volume, originally published some thirty years ago in Swedish. Drawing on collected sayings of the holy men of the East, he presents, for the Western reader, something of the atmosphere of Orthodox spirituality. For Orthodoxy is not primarily a system or a correctness of doctrinal formulations. *Doxa* means glory. Orthodoxy is therefore concerned with "right glory," and it is therefore rooted in the sense of theology as inseparable from human transformation. The purpose of theology is nothing less than the transfiguring of human life "from glory to glory."

At the center of Orthodox theology and spirituality is the theme of *theosis,* deification, the raising of manhood into God. This is the aim of the liturgy, the Eucharistic celebration which stands at the center of all worship and all life. But the centrality of the liturgy is set against the background of what Orthodox theologians describe as "the world as sacrament." The material world is the vehicle, not the enemy, of the spirit. All spirituality has a material basis. As St. John Damascene expressed it, we venerate matter because the Creator of matter "became material" and through matter effected our salvation. So the Creation and the Incarnation are at the heart of Orthodox spiritual disciplines.

This participation in the liturgy, and this sense of the communication of the divine through material things (expressed supremely in the Icons that are so central to Orthodox worship) is taken for granted by the ascetical writers whose thoughts are gathered here. They take for granted too that the Christian disciple who is serious about his or her progress will have a spiritual guide, a *pneumatikos pater* with whom the deepest thoughts of the soul will be shared.

This valuable collection must not be read, then, as a *private* handbook for self-cultivation. The Orthodox spiritual guides are totally opposed to the "privatizing" of religion which is so popular now. They stress the need of the common life, of the sacramental community, of the unity of liturgy and contemplation. They stress too the need for "progress in depth" (Chapter 13) and the place of prayer in the spiritual conflict. Most of all they stress the attainment of "purity of heart," of that inner stillness and silence (*hesychia*) that comes from the practice of the Prayer of Jesus. Through such spiritual discipline, waiting on God in solitude, we come to realize that kinship to God that we, as his images, share.

The rediscovery of Orthodoxy in the West is not only important in terms of the quest for Christian unity. It is essential if we are to recover that lost sense of the mystical and prayerful character of all theology. *All* theology is mystical theology; *all* theology is social theology. For it is rooted in "the life hidden with Christ in God" and in the social life of the Holy Trinity. This unity of the mystical and the social is something we have largely lost in the West, where Christians are often divided into "pietists" and "social activists." The Orthodox know no such distinction. Both the personal life of the "heart" (the Eastern term for the center of the personality) and the corporate life of human society are to be transfigured. So "the way of the ascetics" is not a gloomy, world-denying path; it is a way of *doxa,* of glory, whose aim is nothing less than our deification. This small volume, intended to be read slowly, meditated upon, used and re-used, even learned by heart, can itself become part of our spiritual resources as we move from one degree of glory to another.

KENNETH LEECH

22 July 1981

NOTE

THIS work is based on the holy Fathers of the Orthodox Church and consists largely of direct or freely rendered extracts from their writings, together with some necessary interpretation and practical application.

Scriptural quotations are from the Authorized Version, except those from the Psalms, which follow the Prayer Book Psalter.

Chapter One

ON A RESOLUTE AND SUSTAINED PURPOSE

IF you wish to save your soul and win eternal life, arise from your lethargy, make the sign of the Cross and say:

In the name of the Father, and of the Son and of the Holy Ghost. Amen.

Faith comes not through pondering but through action. Not words and speculation but experience teaches us what God is. To let in fresh air we have to open a window; to get tanned we must go out into the sunshine. Achieving faith is no different; we never reach a goal by just sitting in comfort and waiting, say the holy Fathers. Let the Prodigal Son be our example. He *arose and came* (Luke 15:20).

However weighed down and entangled in earthly fetters you may be, it can never be too late. Not without reason is it written that Abraham was seventy-five when he set forth, and the labourer who comes in the eleventh hour gets the same wages as the one who comes in the first.

Nor can it be too early. A forest fire cannot be put out too soon; would you see your soul ravaged and charred?

In baptism you received the command to wage the invisible warfare against the enemies of your soul; take it up now. Long enough have you dallied; sunk in indifference and laziness you have let much valuable time go to waste. Therefore you must begin again from the beginning: for you have let the purity you received in baptism be sullied in dire fashion.

Arise, then; but do so at once, without delay. Do not defer your purpose till "tonight" or "tomorrow" or "later, when I have finished what I have to do just now." The interval may be fatal.

No, this moment, the instant you make your resolution, you will show by your action that you have taken leave of your old self and have now begun a new life, with a new destination and a new way of living. Arise, therefore, without fear and say: Lord, let me begin now. Help me! For what you need above all is God's help.

Hold fast to your purpose and do not look back. We have been given a warning example in Lot's wife, who was turned into a pillar of salt when she looked back (Genesis 19:26). You have cast off your old humanity; let the rags lie. Like Abraham, you have heard the voice of the Lord: *Get thee out of thy country, and from thy kindred, and from thy father's house, into a land that I will show thee* (Genesis 12:1). Towards that land hereafter you must direct all your attention.

Chapter Two

ON THE INSUFFICIENCY
OF HUMAN STRENGTH

THE holy Fathers say with one voice: The first thing to keep in mind is never in any respect to rely on yourself. The warfare that now lies before you is extraordinarily hard, and your own human powers are altogether insufficient to carry it on. If you rely on them you will immediately be felled to the ground and have no desire to continue the battle. Only God can give you the victory you wish.

This decision not to rely on self is for most people a severe obstacle at the very outset. It must be overcome, otherwise we have no prospect of going further. For how can a human being receive advice, instruction and help if he believes that he knows and can do everything and needs no directions? Through such a wall of self-satisfaction no gleam of light can penetrate. *Woe unto them that are wise in their own eyes, and prudent in their own sight,* cries the prophet Isaiah (5:21), and the apostle St. Paul utters the warning: *Be not wise in your own conceits* (Romans 12:16). The kingdom of heaven has been *revealed unto babes,* but remains hidden from *the wise and prudent* (Matthew 11:25).

We must empty ourselves, therefore, of the immoderately high faith we have in ourselves. Often it is so deeply rooted in us that we do not see how it rules over our heart. It is precisely our egoism, our self-centredness and self-love that cause all our difficulties, our lack of freedom in suffering, our disappointments and our anguish of soul and body.

Take a look at yourself, therefore, and see how bound you are by your desire to humour yourself and only yourself. Your freedom is curbed by the restraining bonds of self-love, and thus you wander, a captive corpse, from morning till eve. "Now I will drink," "now I will get up," "now I will read the paper." Thus you are led from moment to moment in your halter of preoccupation with self, and kindled instantly to displeasure, impatience or anger if an obstacle intervenes.

If you look into the depths of your consciousness you meet the same sight. You recognize it readily by the unpleasant feeling you have when someone contradicts you. Thus we live in thraldom. But *where the Spirit of the Lord is, there is liberty* (II Corinthians 3:17).

How can any good come out of such an orbiting around the ego? Has not our Lord bidden us to love our neighbour as ourselves, and to love God above all? But do we? Are not our thoughts instead always occupied with our own welfare?

No, be convinced that nothing good can come from yourself. And should, by chance, an unselfish thought arise in you, you may be sure that it does not come from you, but is scooped up from the wellspring of goodness and bestowed upon you: it is a gift from the Giver of life. Similarly the power to put the good thought into practice is not your own, but is given you by the Holy Trinity.

Chapter Three

ON THE GARDEN OF THE HEART

HE new life you have just entered has often been likened to that of a gardener. The soil he tills he has received from God, as well as the seed and the sun's warmth and the rain and the power to grow. But the work is entrusted to him.

If the husbandman wishes to have a rich harvest, he must work early and late, weed and aerate, water and spray, for cultivation is beset by many dangers that threaten the harvest. He must work without ceasing, be constantly on the watch, constantly alert, constantly prepared; but even so, the harvest ultimately depends wholly on the elements, that is, on God.

The garden that we have undertaken to tend and watch over is the field of our own heart; the harvest is eternal life.

Eternal, because it is independent of time and space and other external circumstances: it is the true life of freedom, the life of love and mercy and light, that has no bounds whatever, and for just that reason is eternal. It is a spiritual life in a spiritual dominion: a state of being. It begins here, and has no end, and no earthly power can coerce it; and it is to be found in the human heart.

Persecute yourself, says St. Isaac of Syria, and your enemy is routed as fast as you approach. Make peace with yourself, and heaven and earth make peace with you. Take pains to enter your own innermost chamber and you will see the chamber of heaven, for they are one and the same, and in entering one you behold them both. The stairway to the kingdom is within you, secret in your soul. Cast off the burden of sin and you will find within you the upward path that will make your ascent possible.

The heavenly chamber of which the saint speaks here is another name for eternal life. It is also called the kingdom of heaven, the kingdom of God, or quite simply, Christ. To live in Christ is to live in eternal life.

Chapter Four

ON THE SILENT AND INVISIBLE WARFARE

NOW that we know where the battle we have just begun is to be fought, and what and where our goal is, we also understand why our warfare ought to be called the *invisible* warfare. It all takes place in the heart, and in silence, deep within us; and this is another serious matter, on which the holy Fathers lay much stress: keep your lips tight shut on your secret! If one opens the door of the steam bath the heat escapes, and the treatment loses its benefit.

Thus say nothing to anyone of your newly conceived purpose. Say nothing of the new life you have begun or of the experiment you are making and experiences you expect to have. All this is a matter between God and you, and only between you two. The only exception might be your father-confessor.

This silence is necessary because all chatter about one's own concerns nourishes self-preoccupation and self-trust. And these must be stifled first of all! Through stillness one's trust grows in Him who sees what is hidden; through silence one talks with Him who hears without words. To come to Him is your endeavour, and in Him shall be all your confidence: you are anchored in eternity, and in eternity there are no words.

Hereafter you will consider that everything that happens to you, both great and small, is sent by God to help you in your warfare. He alone knows what is necessary for you and what you need at the moment: adversity and prosperity, temptation and fall. Nothing happens accidentally or in such a way that you cannot learn from it; you must understand this at once, for this is how your trust grows in the Lord whom you have chosen to follow.

Still another piece of information the saints offer on the way: you should see yourself as a child who is setting out to learn the first sounds of letters and who is taking his first tottering steps. All worldly wisdom and all the skills you may have are totally worthless in the warfare that awaits you, and equally without value are your social standing and your possessions. Property that is not used in the Lord's service is a burden, and knowledge that does not engage the heart is barren and therefore harmful, because it is presumptuous. It is called naked, for it is without warmth and fosters no love. You must thus abandon all your knowledge and become a dunce in order to be wise; you must become a pauper in order to be rich, and a weakling if you wish to be strong.

Chapter Five

ON THE DENIAL OF SELF AND THE CLEANSING OF THE HEART

NAKED, small and helpless, you now pass on to the most difficult of all human tasks: to conquer your own selfish desires. Ultimately it is just this "self-persecution" on which your warfare depends, for as long as your selfish will rules, you cannot pray to the Lord with a pure heart: *Thy* will be done. If you cannot get rid of your own greatness, neither can you lay yourself open for real greatness. If you cling to your own freedom, you cannot share in true freedom, where only *one* will reigns.

The saints' deep secret is this: do not seek freedom, and freedom will be given you.

The earth brings forth thorns and thistles, it is said. By the sweat of his brow, with anguish shall man till it; it is he himself, his own substance. The holy Fathers' counsel is to begin with small things, for, says Ephraem the Syrian, how can you put out a great fire before you have learned to quench a small one? If you wish to set yourself free from a great suffering, crush the small desires, say the holy Fathers. Do not suppose that the one can be separated from the others: they all hang together like a long chain or a net.

Thus it does not pay to come to grips with the hard-to-master great vices and bad habits you have acquired without at the same time overcoming your small "innocent" weaknesses: your taste for sweets, your urge to talk, your curiosity, your meddling. For, finally, all our desires, great and small, are built on the same foundation, our unchecked habit of satisfying only our own will.

It is the life of our will that is destroyed. Since the Fall the will has been running errands exclusively for its own ego. For this reason our warfare is directed against the life of self-will as such. And it should be undertaken without delay or wearying. If you have the urge to ask something, don't ask! If you have the urge to drink two cups of coffee, drink only one! If you have the urge to look at the clock, don't look! If you wish to smoke a cigarette, refrain! If you want to go visiting, stay at home!

This is self-persecution; in this way does one silence, with God's help, one's loud-voiced will.

You are perhaps wondering, is this really necessary? The holy Fathers reply with another question: Do you really think that you can fill a jar with clean water before the old, dirty water has been emptied out? Or do you wish to receive a beloved guest in a room crammed with old trash and junk? No; he who hopes to see the Lord *as he is, purifies himself,* says the apostle John (I John 3:3).

Thus let us purify our heart! Let us throw out all the dusty trash that is stored there; let us scrub the dirty floor, wash the windows and open them, in order that light and air may come into the room we are preparing as a sanctuary for the Lord. Then let us put on clean garments, so that the old musty smell may not cling to us and we find ourselves *thrust out* (Luke 13:28).

May all this be our daily and hourly travail.

In this way we are only doing what the Lord Himself commanded us through His holy apostle James, who says: *Purify your hearts* (4:8). And the apostle Paul instructs us to *cleanse ourselves from all filthiness of the flesh and spirit* (II Corinthians 7:1). *For from within,* says Christ, *out of the heart of men, proceed evil thoughts, adulteries, fornications, murders, thefts, covetousness, wickedness, deceit, lasciviousness, an evil eye, blasphemy, pride, foolishness. All these evil things come from within, and defile the man* (Mark 7:21–3). Therefore He also exhorts the Pharisees: *Cleanse first that which is within the cup and platter, that the outside of them may be clean also* (Matthew 23:26).

As we now follow instructions to begin with the inside, we must keep in mind that we are not in the least cleansing our heart for our own sake. It is not for our own enjoyment that we furbish and tidy the guest chamber, but in order that the guest may enjoy it. Will he find it pleasant? we ask ourself. Will he stay? Our every thought is for him.

Then we withdraw and keep in the background and expect no recompense.

There are three kinds of nature in man, as Nicetas Stethatos further explains: the carnal man, who wants to live for his own pleasure, even if it harms others; the natural man, who wants to please both himself and others; and the spiritual man, who wants to please only God, even if it harms himself.

The first is lower than human nature, the second is normal, the third is above nature; it is life in Christ.

Spiritual man thinks spiritually; his hope is sometime to hear the angels' joy *over one sinner that repenteth* (Luke 15:10), and that sinner is himself. Such should be your feeling, and in this hope you should labour, for the Lord has bidden us *be perfect even as your Father which is in Heaven is perfect* (Matthew 5:48), and to *seek first the kingdom of God and his righteousness* (6:33).

Therefore give yourself no rest, allow yourself no peace until you have slain that part within you that belongs to your carnal nature. Make it your purpose to track down every sign of the bestial within you and persecute it relentlessly. *For the flesh lusteth against the Spirit and the Spirit against the flesh* (Galatians 5:17).

But if you are fearful of becoming self-righteous from working for your own salvation, or afraid of being overcome by spiritual pride, examine yourself and observe that the person who is afraid of *becoming* self-righteous suffers from blindness. For he does not see how self-righteous he *is*.

Chapter Six

ON ERADICATING THE DESIRE FOR ENJOYMENT

I T is said that only a few find the narrow way that leads to life and that we must strive to enter by the narrow door. *For many, I say unto you, will seek to enter in, and shall not be able* (Luke 13:24).

The explanation is to be found precisely in our unwillingness to persecute ourselves. We overcome after a fashion, perhaps, our serious and dangerous vices, but there it stops. The small desires we freely let grow as they will. We neither embezzle nor steal, but delight in gossiping; we do not "drink," but consume immoderate quantities of tea and coffee instead. The heart remains quite as full of appetites: the roots are not pulled out and we wander around in the tanglewoods that have sprung up in the soil of our self-pity.

Make an onslaught on your self-pity, for it is the root of all ill that befalls you. If you were not full of self-pity you would soon observe that we ourselves are to blame for all this evil, because we refuse to understand that it is in reality a good thing. Commiserating yourself obscures your sight. You are compassionate only for yourself and as a result your horizon closes in. Your love is bound up with yourself. Set it free and evil departs from you.

Suppress your ruinous weakness and your craving for comfort; attack them from every side! Crush your desire for enjoyment; do not give it air to breathe. Be strict with yourself; do not grant your carnal ego the bribes it is restively demanding. For everything gains strength from repetition, but dies if it is not given nourishment.

But take care not to bar the front entrance to evil and at the same time leave a back door ajar, through which it can cleverly slip in in another form.

How do you benefit if, for example, you begin to sleep on a hard mattress but instead indulge in warm baths? Or if you try to give up smoking but give free rein to your urge to prattle? Or if you deny your urge to prattle, but read exciting novels? Or if you stop reading novels but let loose your imagination and quiver in sweet melancholy?

All these are only different forms of the same thing: your insatiable craving to satisfy your own need for enjoyment.

You must set about rooting out the very desire to have things pleasant, to get on well, to be contented. You must learn to like sadness, poverty, pain, hardship. You must learn to follow privately the Lord's bidding: not to speak empty words, not to adorn yourself, always to obey authority, not to look at a woman with desire, not to be angry and much else. For all these biddings are given us not in order for us to act as if they did not exist, but for us to follow: otherwise the Lord of mercy would not have burdened us with them. *If any man will come after me, let him deny himself,* He said (Matthew 16:24), thereby leaving it to each person's own will—if any man *will*—and to each person's endeavour: let him deny *himself.*

Chapter Seven

ON THE TRANSFER OF LOVE FROM THE SELF TO CHRIST

I F we move out of our self, whom do we encounter? asks Bishop Theophan. He supplies the answer at once: We meet God and our neighbour. It is for this very reason that *denying oneself* is a stipulation, and the chief one, for the person who seeks salvation in Christ: only so can the centre of our being be moved from self to Christ, who is both God and our neighbour.

This means that all the care, concern and love that we now lavish on ourselves is then quite naturally and without our noticing it transferred to God and thereby to our fellowmen. Only so is the left hand kept from knowing *what thy right hand doeth,* and *your alms* are actually given *in secret* (Matthew 6:3–4).

Until this has come to pass, we cannot *be filled with all knowledge, able also to admonish one another* (Romans 15:14) in a real, non-material way. Our attempts along this line must be false because they are our own and spring from our will to please ourselves. It is especially necessary to understand this, for otherwise we become easily confused on the road of specious helpfulness and smug well-meaning that leads inevitably to the swamp of self-satisfaction.

Refrain from busying yourself, therefore, with charity bazaars, sewing meetings and other such occupations. Busyness over many things is, in all its forms, chiefly a poison. Look within, examine yourself accurately, and you observe that many of these apparently self-giving deeds spring from a need to deafen your conscience: that is, from your uncontrollable habit of satisfying and pleasing yourself (Romans 15:1).

No, the God of love and peace and complete sacrifice does not care to live in the midst of bustling and ado to please oneself, even if this is carried on perhaps under some kind of pretence. There is one way to make a test: if your peace of mind is troubled, if you become dejected or perhaps a little angry if for some reason you have to give up performing the good deed you had planned, then you know that the spring was muddy.

Perhaps you ask, Why? Those who are experienced answer, external hindrance and opposition meet only the person who has not yielded his own will to God: and for God an obstacle is unthinkable. A truly unselfish act is not mine, but God's. It cannot be obstructed. Only for my own plans, my own wishes—to study, to work, to rest, eat, or do a service to my fellowman—can some external circumstance "get in the way," and then I am grieved. But for the person who has found the narrow way *that leads to life,* that is to God, there is only one conceivable hindrance, and that is his own, sinful will. If he now wishes to do something but is not permitted to carry it out, how can he grieve? For the rest he is not making any plans (James 4:13–16).

But this is another of the saints' secrets.

Do not be deceived. A Christian *ought himself also so to walk, even as he walked* (I John 2:6) who did not seek his own will (John 5:30), but, was born on straw, fasted forty days, watched in prayer long nights through, healed the sick, drove out evil spirits, had no place to lay his head, and who finally let himself be spat upon, scourged and crucified.

Think how far you are from that. Ask yourself continually anew: Have I watched in prayer a single night? Have I fasted a single day? Have I driven out a single evil spirit? Have I unresistingly let myself be insulted and beaten? Have I truly *crucified the flesh* (Galatians 5:24), and not sought my own will?

Keep all this freshly in mind.

For what is denying oneself? He who truly denies himself does not ask, Am I happy? or, Shall I be satisfied? All such questions fall away from you if you truly deny yourself, for by so doing you have also given up your will for either earthly or heavenly happiness.

This obstinate will to personal happiness is the cause of unrest and division in your soul. Give it up and work against it: the rest will be given you without effort.

Chapter Eight

ON GUARDING AGAINST THE RE-ENTRY OF VANQUISHED EVIL

HE first time you are victorious over self may be a sign to you: Now I am on the way! But do not consider yourself virtuous, only thank God, for it was He who gave you the power; and do not rejoice beyond measure, but swiftly go on. Otherwise the vanquished evil may come to life and conquer you from the rear. Remember: the Israelites received the command from God to *drive out all the inhabitants of the land* when they conquered the new land (Numbers 33:52f.), in order that we might learn from them.

The degree of victory over self is of trifling importance. It consisted perhaps in our skipping our morning cigarette, or only in such an apparently unimportant thing as not turning our head or refraining from meeting a glance. The externally noticeable happening is not the decisive one. The little thing can be big, and the big, little. But always the next phase of the battle is already waiting. We must be constantly prepared. There is no time to rest.

Once again, be silent! Let no one notice what you are about. You are working for the Invisible One; let your work be invisible. If you scatter crumbs around you they are willingly picked up by birds sent by the devil, the saints explain. Beware of self-satisfaction: in one mouthful it can devour the fruit of much toil.

Therefore the Fathers counsel: act with discernment. Of two evils one chooses the lesser. If you are in private, take the poorest morsel, but if anyone is looking, you should take the middle way that arouses the least notice. Keep hidden and as inconspicuous as possible; in all circumstances let this be your rule. Do not talk about yourself, of how you slept, what you dreamed and what happened to you, do not state your views unasked, do not touch upon your own wants and concerns. All such talk only nourishes your self-preoccupation.

Do not change your work, your residence,

and the like. Remember: there is no place, no community, no external circumstance that is not serviceable for the battle you have chosen. The exception is only such work as directly serves your vices.

Do not seek higher posts and higher titles: the lower the position of service you have, the freer you are. Be satisfied with the living conditions you now have. And do not be prompt to show your learning or skill. Hold back your remarks, No, it isn't so-and-so, but so-and-so. Contradict nobody and do not get into arguments; let the other person always be right. Never set your own will above that of your neighbour. This teaches you the difficult art of submission, and along with it, humility. Humility is indispensable.

Take remarks without grumbling: be thankful when you are scorned, disregarded, ignored. But do not create humbling situations; they are provided in the course of the day as richly as you need. We notice the person who is for ever bowing and fussily servile, and perhaps say, How humble he is! But the truly humble person escapes notice: the world does not know him (I John 3:1); for the world he is mostly a "zero."

When Peter and Andrew, John and James *left their nets and followed him* (Matthew 4:20) what did their fellow workers say, who were left on the shore? For them the two pairs of brothers vanished; they were gone. Do not be hesitant; do not be afraid of disappearing like them, from *this adulterous and sinful generation;* what are you hoping to win, the world or your soul (Mark 8:34–38)? *Woe to you, when all men shall speak well of you* (Luke 6:26).

Chapter Nine

ON THE CONQUEST
OF THE WORLD

T. BASIL the Great says: One cannot approach the knowledge of the truth with a disturbed heart. Therefore we must try to avoid everything that disturbs our heart, that causes forgetfulness, excitement or passion, or that awakens unrest. We must free ourselves as much as possible from all fuss and flutter and ado over vain things. Yes, when we serve the Lord we shall not be *troubled about many things,* but always keep in mind that *one thing is needful* (Luke 10:41).

In order to bathe one must first undress. So it is with the heart: it must be set free from the world's outer covering in order to be accessible to the Cleanser. The healthful rays of the sun cannot reach the skin if we do not first uncover it and stand naked. So it is with the Spirit's healing and life-giving power.

Thus: undress. Deny yourself, but without it being too noticeable, everything that contributes to enjoyment and pleasure, comfort or entertainment, everything that is amusing or caresses the eyes, ears, palate or other senses. *He that is not with me is against me* (Matthew 12:30), and what does not build up, tears down. Peel off your every day needs and social habits: do so calmly, deliberately, without too sudden transition, yet thoroughly. Gradually clip off as many strings as possible that bind you to the external world: invitations, concerts, personal property, and especially *all that is in the world, the lust of the flesh and the lust of the eyes and the pride of life,* for it *is not of the Father but is of the world,* and it wages war against your soul (I John 2:16).

What is the world, then? You ought not to imagine it as something sinful and tangible. The world, explains St. Macarius of Egypt, is the veil of dark flames that surround the heart and shut it out from the tree of life. The world is everything that holds us and satisfies us sensuously: that within us which has not known God (John 17:25).

To the world belong our desires and impulses. St. Isaac the Syrian enumerates them: Weakness for wealth and for collecting and owning things of different kinds; the urge for physical (sensuous) enjoyment; the longing for honour, which is the root of envy; the desire to conquer and be the deciding factor; pride in the glory of power; the urge to adorn oneself and to be liked; the craving for praise; concern and anxiety for physical well-being. All these are of the world; they combine deceitfully to hold us in heavy bonds.

If you wish to free yourself, scrutinize yourself with the help of that list and see clearly what you have to struggle against in order to approach God. For *friendship with the world is enmity with God,* and *whosoever therefore will be a friend of the world is the enemy of God* (James 4:4). Broad vistas are attained only by leaving the narrow valley and the occupations and pleasures characteristic of the valley. *No man can serve two masters* (Matthew 6:24); to sojourn at the same time in the valley and on the heights is impossible.

To ease the upward climb and the more readily cast off the heavy burdens, you can as often as possible ask yourself such questions, for example, as these: Is it for *my own* or for someone else's pleasure that I am now going to this concert or to the cinema? Am I crucifying my flesh at a cocktail party? Am I going and selling all I possess by taking a pleasure trip or buying this book? Am I *keeping under my body and bringing it into subjection* (I Corinthians 9:27) by lying down to read? The questions can be altered and added to according to your own habits and their relation to the way of life the Gospel commands. Thereupon you should remember that *he that is faithful in that which is least is faithful also in much* (Luke 16:10). And do not fear the pain; it helps you out of the narrow valley, where you lived in the passions of your flesh, following the desires of body and mind (Ephesians 2:3).

Without mercy you should ask yourself such questions continually and incessantly. But ask them of yourself only. Never in any case, not even in thought, of another. As soon as you direct such a question outward to your fellow man and not inward to yourself, you have set yourself on a judgment seat and thereby judged yourself. You have robbed yourself of what

you had won by your own continence; you
have taken one step forward but ten backward:
and then you have reason to weep over your
obstinacy, your failure to improve, and your
pride.

Chapter Ten

ON THE SINS OF OTHERS
AND ONE'S OWN

NOW that you have thus become aware of your own wretchedness, your insufficiency, and your wickedness, you call upon the Lord as did the Publican (Luke 18:13): *God, be merciful to me a sinner.* And you add: Behold, I am far worse than the Publican, for I cannot resist eyeing the Pharisee askance, and my heart is proud and says: I thank Thee that I am not like him!

But, say the saints, now that you recognize the darkness in your own heart and the weakness of your flesh, you lose all desire to pass judgment on your neighbour. Out of your own darkness you see the heavenly light that shines in all created things reflected the clearer: you

cannot detect the sins of others while your own
are so great. For it is in your eager striving for
perfection that you first perceive your own imperfection. And only when you have seen your
imperfection, can you be perfected. Thus perfection proceeds out of weakness.

At this point you are granted the result that
Isaac the Syrian promises to those who persecute themselves: And your enemy is driven off
as fast as you approach.

Of what enemy is the holy Father speaking
here? Naturally, of the same one who once took
the shape of a serpent and who, ever since,
arouses discontent in us, dissatisfaction, impatience and impetuosity and anger, envy, fear,
anguish, anxiety, hate, dispiritedness, laziness,
dejection, doubt and especially all that embitters
our existence and that has its roots in our self-
love and self-pity.

For who can wish to be obeyed who realizes,
with the pangs of love, that he himself never
obeys his Master? What reason, then, has he to
be disturbed, to become impatient and impas-
sioned, if everything does not go according to
his wishes? Through practice he has accustomed
himself to wish for nothing, and for a person
with no wishes, everything goes just as he
wishes, explains the Abbot Dorotheus. His will

has coincided with God's will, and whatever he
asks, he will receive (Mark 11:24).

Can one very well be envious of a person
who does not exalt himself, but who, on the
contrary, sees his own condition and finds that
everyone else is far more worthy of fame and
honour than he? Are fear, anguish and anxiety
possible for the person who knows that, come
what may, he, like the robber on the cross, is
receiving the due reward of his deeds (Luke 23:
41)? Laziness leaves him because he is constantly unmasking it within himself. Dejection
finds no place, for how can what is already
prostrate be cast down? And his hate is directed
exclusively towards all the evil in his own life
that dims his view of the Lord: he hates his own
life (Luke 14:26). But then there is no longer
any ground for doubt, for he has tasted and
seen how gracious the Lord is (Psalm 34:8): it is
the Lord alone who bears him up. His love
grows constantly in breadth, and with it his
faith.

He has made peace with himself, as Isaac the
Syrian says, and heaven and earth have made
peace with him. He is gathering the fruit of
humility. But this takes place only on the narrow way, and *few there be that find it* (Matthew
7:14).

Chapter Eleven

ON THE INNER WARFARE
AS A MEANS TO AN END

B Y throwing off the outer bonds, you throw off the inner as well. While you are freeing yourself from external concerns, your heart is freed from inner pain. It follows from this that the hard warfare you are compelled to wage with yourself is exclusively a means. As such it is neither good nor bad; the saints often liken it to a prescribed cure. However painful it may be to follow out, it nevertheless remains only a means to regain health.

Always keep this in mind: you are not doing anything virtuous by your continence. Or can it be considered a virtuous act when a man who, out of his own carelessness, has been trapped deep down in a mine shaft, takes pick and shovel and tries to work his way out? Is it not, on the contrary, quite natural for him to make use of the tools given him by a higher authority to make his way up out of the choking air and darkness? Would not the opposite be stupidity?

From this picture you can gain wisdom. The tools are the implements of salvation, the commands of the Gospel and the holy Sacraments of the Church, that were bestowed upon every Christian at holy baptism. Unused, they are of no profit to you. But used in the right manner they will open your way to freedom and light.

We must through much tribulation enter into the kingdom of God (Acts 14:22): we must, like the imprisoned victim, give up many opportunities for rest and sleep and enjoyment; we must, like him, watch and employ every moment when others sleep or occupy themselves with trifling things. We do not let the pick and shovel out of our hands: they are prayer, fasting, watching and work to *observe all things whatsoever I have commanded you* (Matthew 28:20). Further, if the heart finds such discipline difficult, we must use all our will-power to compel it to submit if we are to get out.

What reward does the prisoner get now? Or does he get any reward at all?

Toil itself is his reward. In the love of freedom that he feels, in the hope and faith that placed the tools in his hands. With work, hope and love and faith grow: the more industrious he is, and the less he spares himself, the greater is his reward. He becomes aware of himself as a prisoner among prisoners, in his own eyes he does not separate himself from his comrades: he is a sinner among sinners in the bowels of the earth. But while they, in hopeless resignation, sleep or play cards to while away the time, he goes forth to his work. He has found a treasure but he covers it up (Matthew 13:44); he carries the kingdom of heaven within him: love, hope and the faith that sometime he will reach the fresh air outside. As yet, to be sure, he sees true freedom only in a mirror (I Corinthians 13:12), but in hope he is already free: *We are saved by hope* (Romans 8:24). *But hope that is seen is not hope,* adds the apostle, in order that we might rightly understand what is involved. Once the prisoner really reaches freedom and sees it face to face, he is no longer a prisoner among prisoners on earth. Then he finds that he is already in the world of freedom: the freedom in which Adam was created and which was restored to us in Christ.

Like the prisoner, we are already free in

hope, but the fulfillment of salvation lies beyond our earthly life: only there can we say definitely: I am saved. For the command to be perfect as your heavenly Father is perfect (Matthew 5:48) is impossible of human fulfillment here on earth. Why was it given to us, then? The saints reply: In order that we might begin our work now, but with eternity before our eyes.

The goal of man's freedom is neither in himself nor in his fellow man but in God, says Bishop Theophan.

For the cry of freedom is: Repent! And the call is given: *Come unto me all ye that labour and are heavy-laden, and I will give you rest* (Matthew 11:28f.). *Labour* on what? On your own temporal welfare? Are *heavy-laden*—with what? With earthly cares and concerns? Not in the least, reply the saints. For what does the Lord go on to say: *Take my yoke upon you and learn of me,* who never thought of my temporal welfare and never was burdened with worldly cares while I wandered on earth.

And what do they get, all those who labour on their salvation and are heavy-laden with the world's opposition, both within themselves and without? Those who take Christ's yoke upon themselves and live as He lived, and therefore learn not from angels nor from men nor from books, but from the Lord Himself, from His own life and light and action within them; who too can say I am meek and lowly in heart and hold no high opinion either of myself or of what I do or say or can do—what do all these people get? They will find rest for their souls. The Lord Himself will give them rest. They will receive freedom from temptations, worries, humiliations, spite, fear, anxiety and everything else that disturbs the human heart.

This is the explanation of St. John Climacus. And so it has spread from Christian to Christian. For experience reveals again and again to the new heart the truth that Christ's yoke is easy and his burden is light for those who love Him.

But only *he that endureth to the end shall be saved* (Matthew 10:22), not those who fall away and are lazy. The promise does not concern them.

Therefore we must not grow weary. We must be steadfast, immovable, always abounding in the work of the Lord, knowing that in the Lord our labour is not in vain (I Corinthians

15:58). Having once begun, we must not cease to perform deeds worthy of our repentance. To rest is the same as to retreat.

Chapter Twelve

ON OBEDIENCE

BEDIENCE is another indispensable implement in the struggle against our selfish will. With obedience you cut off your physical members the better to be able to serve with the spiritual, says St. John Climacus. And again, obedience is the grave of your own will, but from it rises humility.

You must remember that you have of your own free will given yourself over to slavery, and let the cross you wear around your neck be a reminder of this: through slavery you are proceeding towards true freedom. But has the slave a will of his own? He must learn to obey.

Perhaps you ask: Whom shall I obey? The saints answer: you shall obey your leaders (Hebrews 13:17). Who are my leaders, you ask? Where shall I find any, now that it is so utterly hard to discover a genuine leader? Then the holy Fathers reply: The Church has foreseen this too. Therefore since the time of the apostles it has given us a teacher who surpasses all others and who can reach us everywhere, wherever we are and under whatever circumstances we live. Whether we be in city or country, married or single, poor or rich, the teacher is always with us and we always have the opportunity to show him obedience. Do you wish to know his name? It is holy fasting.

God does not need our fasting. He does not even need our prayer. The Perfect cannot be thought of as suffering any lack or needing anything that we, the creatures of His making, could give Him. Nor does he crave anything from us, but, says John Chrysostom, He allows us to bring Him offerings for the sake of our own salvation.

The greatest offering we can present to the Lord is our self. We cannot do this without giving up our own will. We learn to do this through obedience, and obedience we learn through practice. The best form of practice is that provided by the Church in her prescribed fast days and seasons.

Besides fasting we have other teachers to

whom we can show obedience. They meet us at
every step in our daily life, if only we recognize
their voices. Your wife wants you to take your
raincoat with you: do as she wishes, to practise
obedience. Your fellow-worker asks you to
walk with her a little way: go with her to practise obedience. Wordlessly the infant asks for
care and companionship: do as it wishes as far
as you can, and thus practise obedience. A nov-
ice in a cloister could not find more opportunity
for obedience than you in your own home. And
likewise at your job and in your dealings with
your neighbour.

Obedience breaks down many barriers. You
achieve freedom and peace as your heart practises non-resistance. You show obedience, and
thorny hedges give way before you. Then love
has open space in which to move about. By
obedience you crush your pride, your desire to
contradict, your self-wisdom and stubbornness
that imprison you within a hard shell. Inside
that shell you cannot meet the God of love and
freedom.

Thus, make it a habit to rejoice when an opportunity for obedience offers. It is quite un-
necessary to seek one, for you may easily fall
into a studied servility that leads you astray into

self-righteous virtue. You may depend upon it that you are sent just as many opportunities for obedience as you need, and the very kind that are most suitable for you. But if you notice that you have let an opportunity slip by, reproach yourself; you have been like a sailor who has let a favourable wind go by unused.

For the wind it was a matter of indifference whether it was used or not. But for the sailor it was a means of reaching his destination sooner. Thus you should think of obedience, and all the means that are offered us by the Holy Trinity, in that way.

Chapter Thirteen

ON PROGRESS
IN DEPTH

THE external rudiments lead us now to the welfare that goes on in the depths. As when one peels an onion, one layer after another is removed, and the innermost core, out of which growth reaches up toward the light, lies revealed. There, in your own innermost chamber, you will glimpse the heavenly chamber, for they are one and the same, according to St. Isaac the Syrian.

When you strive now to enter your inmost depths, you will be aware, beside your own true face, of what St. Hesychius of Jerusalem calls the gloomy faces of thought's Ethiopians, but what St. Macarius of Egypt likens to a crawling serpent that has nestled there and wounded your soul's most vital organ. If now you have slain this serpent, he says, you may pride yourself on your purity before God. But if you have not, bow humbly, as a needy sinner, and pray to God about all that lurks within you.

How can we make a beginning, then, we who have never penetrated into the heart? We stand outside, but let us knock with fasting and prayer, as the Lord commands when He says: *Knock and it shall be opened unto you* (Matthew 7:7). For to knock is to act. And if we stand fast in the word of the Lord, in poverty, in humility, in all that the injunctions of the Gospel require, and night and day hammer upon God's spiritual door, then we shall be able to get what we seek. Whoever will escape darkness and captivity can walk out into freedom through that door. There he receives the disposition to spiritual freedom, and the possibility of reaching Christ, the heavenly King, says St. Macarius.

Chapter Fourteen

ON HUMILITY AND WATCHFULNESS

WHOEVER engages in inner warfare needs at every moment four things: humility, the greatest vigilance, the will to resist and prayer. It is a matter of dominating, with God's help, the "Ethiopians of thought," thrusting them out by the door of the heart, and crushing at once those who dash your little ones against the rocks (Psalm 137:9).

Humility is a prerequisite, for the proud man is once and for all shut out. Vigilance is necessary in order immediately to recognize the enemies and to keep the heart free from vice. The will to resist must be established at the very instant the enemy is recognized. But since *without me ye can do nothing* (John 15:5), prayer is the basis on which the whole battle depends.

A little example may be of guidance to you.

By being vigilant you discover an enemy approaching the door of your heart, for example, the temptation to think an evil thought of a fellow man. Immediately your will to resist is awakened and you thrust out the temptation, but at the very next moment you sustain a setback in the form of a self-satisfied thought: My, but I was alert! Your apparent victory became a horrible defeat. Humility was missing.

If, on the contrary, you give over the battle to your Lord, the tendency to self-satisfaction falls away and you stand free. Soon you observe, too, that there is no weapon so powerful as the name of the Lord.

The example shows how unremittingly the warfare must be carried on. In a swift stream the evil impulses flow in, and they must be checked as quickly as possible. These are *all the fiery darts of the wicked* of which the apostle speaks (Ephesians 6:16), and that come flying without cessation. Without cessation, therefore, must also be our cry to the Lord. Our fight is not a fight *against flesh and blood, but against principalities, against powers, against the darkness of this world, against spiritual wickedness in high places* (Ephesians 6:12).

The *impulse* is the beginning, the saints explain. Then *intercourse* * follows, when we enter further into what the impulse brings with it. The third step is already *consent,* and the fourth is the committed *sin.* These four stages can succeed each other instantly, but they can also give way by degrees so that one can manage to separate them. The impulse knocks like a salesman at the door. If one lets him in, he begins his sales talk about his wares, and it is hard to get rid of him even if one observes that the wares are not good. Thus follow consent and finally the purchase, often against one's own will. One has let himself be led astray by what the evil one has sent.

Of impulses David says: *I shall soon destroy all the unholy that are in the land* (Psalm 101:11), for *there shall no deceitful person dwell in my house* (v. 10). And of consent, Moses says, *Thou shalt make no covenant with them* (Exodus 23:32). The first verse of Psalm I also treats the same thing, say the Fathers: *Blessed is the man that hath not walked in the counsel of the ungodly . . . .* It is thus of great importance to speak with his enemies *in the gate* (Psalm 127:5).

---

*The technical term is in Greek *syndyasmos,* and in Latin *conjunctio.*

But when the throng at the gate is large, and when we know that *Satan himself is transformed into an angel of light* (II Corinthians 11:14), the holy Fathers advise us to keep the heart pure from all impulses, feelings and fantasies of whatever kind they may be. That is to say, it is not within human power to separate evil impulses from good ones: the Lord alone can do that. So we relinquish the matter with confidence to Him, well knowing that *unless the Lord keep the city, the watchman waketh but in vain* (Psalm 127:2).

It depends on you, nevertheless, to take heed lest there be a base thought in your heart (Deuteronomy 15:9), and to see to it that your heart does not become a market place where like and unlike gather in a continual tumult, until you completely lose sight of what is happening. Here thieves and robbers hold their tryst, but never the angel of peace you need. Peace, and with it the Lord of peace, flees from such a place.

Therefore He has told us through His apostle: *Purify your hearts* (James 4:8) and instructed us Himself: *Take ye heed, watch and pray* (Mark 13:33). For if He comes and finds our hearts impure and us asleep, He says: *I know you not*

(Matthew 25:12). But the hour is always here, if not at this moment, then at the next; and if not at the next, then at this. For like the kingdom of heaven, the hour of judgment is always present in our heart.

Thus, if the watchman does not watch, neither does the Lord watch; but if the Lord does not watch, the watchman watches in vain. Let us, therefore, watch at the door of our heart, while never ceasing to call upon the Lord for help.

Do not direct your gaze towards the enemy. Never get into a controversy with him whom you cannot possibly resist. With his millennia of experience he knows the very trick that can render you helpless at once. No, stand in the middle of your heart's field and keep your gaze upward; then the heart is protected from all sides at once: the Lord Himself sends His angels to guard it both from right and left and from the rear at the same time.

This, being interpreted, means that if you are beset by a temptation, you should not consider it a matter for examination or reflection or weighing for or against: by so doing you sully your heart and waste time, and already it is a victory for the enemy. Instead, without the slightest delay, turn to the Lord and say: Lord, have mercy on me, a sinner. And the sooner you draw your thoughts away from the temptation, the sooner help comes.

Never be sure of yourself. Never make a good resolution, and never think: Oh yes, I'll make out all right. Never believe in your own power and strength to resist temptation of any kind, great or small. Think, on the contrary: I am sure to fall as soon as it comes upon me. Self-confidence is a dangerous confederate. The less strength you credit yourself with, the more surely you stand. Acknowledge that you are weak, completely unable to resist the slightest beckoning of the devil. Then to your astonishment you will find that he has no power over you. For if you have made the Lord your refuge you will soon be able to ensure that no evil shall befall you (Psalm 91). The only evil that can befall a Christian is sin.

If you are remorseful because later on you fell anyway, and if you are full of self-reproach and resolutions "never to do so again," it is a sure sign that you are on the wrong road: it is your self-reliance that has been wounded.

He who does not rely on himself is thankfully amazed that he did not fall lower; he praises God for sending him help in time, for otherwise he would still have been lying prostrate. Swiftly he rises and begins his prayer with a threefold *Praised be God*.

A spoiled child lies smarting for a long time when it has fallen. It seeks sympathy and comforting caresses. Do not fuss over yourself, no matter how it hurts. Get up again and resume the battle. He who fights gets wounded. Only angels never fall.

But pray God to forgive you and not again to allow you to be unwary.

Do not follow Adam's example and place the blame on the woman or the devil or on any other external circumstance. The reason for your fall lay within yourself: in the moment when the Master of the house was away from your heart, you let thieves and robbers come in and make havoc there at will. Pray God that this be not repeated.

A monk was once asked: What do you do there in the monastery? He replied: We fall and get up, fall and get up, fall and get up again.

For not many minutes of your life go by

without your having fallen at least once. Thus pray God to have mercy on us all.

Pray for forgiveness and grace, and for mercy as a criminal sentenced to death prays, and remember that it is only *by grace ye are saved* (Ephesians 2:5). You can make no claim whatever to freedom and grace. Think of yourself as in the position of a runaway slave as he lies before his lord, praying to be spared. Such shall your prayer be, if you will follow St. Isaac the Syrian and "cast off your burden of sin within yourself," in order to find there "the upward path that makes ascent possible."

Chapter Fifteen

ON PRAYER

T follows from this that *prayer* is your first and incomparably most important means of fighting. Learn to pray, and you vanquish all the evil powers that could imaginably assail you.

Prayer is one wing, faith the other, that lifts us heavenward. With only one wing no one can fly: prayer without faith is as meaningless as faith without prayer. But if your faith is very weak, you can profitably cry: Lord, give me faith! Such a prayer seldom goes unheard. The grain of mustard seed, says the Lord, grows into a great tree.

The person who wants sunshine and air opens the window. It would be folly to sit behind drawn curtains and say: There is no light; there isn't a breath of air! Let this picture show you clearly how prayer works. God's power, or grace, is always and everywhere accessible to all, but one cannot get one's share of it without wanting it and acting accordingly.

Prayer is action; to pray is to be highly effective. For every kind of effectiveness needs practice. It is by speaking a foreign language that one learns it, and by praying one learns to pray.

Without prayer you can never expect to find what you are seeking. Prayer is the beginning and the basis of all striving towards God. The first gleam of light is lit by prayer; prayer gives the first hints of what you are seeking, and it awakens and sustains the desire to go further.

Prayer is the foundation of the world, St. John Climacus has said, and another saint has likened the universe to a bowl in which the Church of Christ rests, but the Church is held together by prayer. Prayer is humanity's intercourse and encounter with God. It is the bridge on which man crosses over from his carnal self with its temptations, to the spiritual, with its freedom. It is a wall of defence against troubles, a weapon against doubt; it annihilates affliction and bridles anger. Prayer is food for the soul and light for the mind, it bears in the present the joy that is to come. For him who truly prays, prayer is the verdict, the tribunal, and the Judge's throne, not waiting for the Last Judgment, but now, in the next moment, in the heart.

Prayer and watchfulness are one and the same, for it is with prayer that you stand at the gate of your heart. The watchful eye reacts immediately to the slightest shifting in the field of vision; so also does the heart that is steadfast in prayer.

The spider may be another example for you. In the middle of his web he sits and feels the smallest fly and kills it. Likewise prayer watches in the middle of your heart: as soon as a trembling makes it known that an enemy is there, prayer kills it.

To leave off praying is the same thing as deserting one's post. The gate stands open for the ravaging hordes, and the treasures one has gathered are plundered. The plunderer does not need long to accomplish his work: anger, for example, can destroy everything in a single second.

Chapter Sixteen

ON PRAYER

FROM the foregoing we understand that by prayer the holy Fathers are not referring to occasional prayer, morning and evening devotions and grace at meals, but for them prayer is synonymous with unceasing prayer, the life of prayer. *Pray without ceasing* (I Thessalonians 5:17) is to be taken as a literal command.

Understood in this way, prayer is the science of scientists and the art of artists. The artist works in clay or colours, in word or tones; according to his ability he gives them pregnancy and beauty. The working material of the praying person is living humanity. By his prayer he shapes it, gives it pregnancy and beauty: first himself and thereby many others.

The man of science studies created things and

appearances; the man of prayer presses through to the Creator of created things. It is not warmth that induces his love, but the well-spring of warmth; not the functions of life, but the origin of life; not his own ego but the source of consciousness in an ego: the Creator of it.

The artist and the scientist must put in much labour and toil before they reach maturity. The skill they desire they never attain. If they were to wait for divine inspiration every time they go to work, they would never learn the principles of their profession. The violinist must practise perseveringly in order to be initiated into the secrets of his sensitive instrument. How much more sensitive is the human heart!

Draw nigh to God and he will draw nigh to you (James 4:8). It is for us to begin. If we take one step toward the Lord, He takes ten toward us—He who saw the Prodigal Son while he was yet at a distance, and had compassion and ran and embraced him (Luke 15:20).

Some time you must take the first uncertain steps—if you wish at all to draw near to God. Do not be anxious about your clumsy beginning; do not yield to shyness and uncertainty, and the mocking laughter of enemies, who try to persuade you that you are behaving ridiculously and that the whole thing is only a child of fantasy and meaningless. Know that there is nothing the enemy fears like prayer.

The child's desire to read increases as he learns to read; the further one gets into a language, the better he speaks it and the more he likes it. Enjoyment increases with proficiency. Proficiency comes with practice. Practice becomes more pleasant as proficiency increases.

Do not suppose that it is otherwise with prayer. Do not wait for some extraordinary divine inspiration before setting to work. Man is created for prayer just as he is created to speak and to think. But especially for prayer; for the Lord God put man *into the garden of Eden to dress it and to keep it* (Genesis 2:15). And where will you find the garden of Eden if not in your heart?

Like Adam, you ought to weep for the Eden of which you were deprived because of your incontinence. You were clad in fig leaves and garments of skin (Genesis 3:21), that is your perishable substance with its suffering. Between you and the narrow way to the tree of life lay the dark flames of earthly desires, and only to him who conquers these desires will it be given

*to eat of the tree of life, which is in the midst of the
paradise of God* (Revelation 2:7).

How hard it is to win such a victory! Adam
broke only one of the Lord's commandments;
daily and hourly you break them all, says St.
Andrew of Crete. From your position as a
hardened, constant criminal your prayer must
go forth, in order to reach the heights.

The hardened criminal often is not conscious
of his guilt; he is hardened. So it is with us. Do
not let yourself be frightened by the hardness of
your own heart. Prayer will gradually soften it.

Chapter Seventeen

ON PRAYER

A PERSON who resolves to begin regular morning exercises usually does so not because he already *has* physical fitness but in order to get something he *does not have*. Once one has something he can be anxious to keep it; previous to that, he is anxious to get it.

Therefore, begin your practice without expecting anything of yourself. If you are fortunate enough to sleep in a room by yourself, you can quite literally and without trouble follow the instructions of the prayer book:

"When you awake, before you begin the day, stand with reverence before the All-Seeing God. Make the sign of the Cross and say:

"In the Name of the Father, and of the Son, and of the Holy Ghost. Amen.

"Having invoked the Holy Trinity, keep silence for a little, so that your thoughts and feelings may be freed from worldly cares. Then recite the following prayers without haste, and with your whole heart.

"God, be merciful to me, a sinner."

Thereafter follow the other prayers,* with the prayer to the Holy Spirit first, then to the Holy Trinity, and next the Our Father, which precedes the whole list of morning prayers. It is better to read a few of them quietly than all of them impatiently. They rest upon the gathered experience of the Church; through them you enter a great fellowship of praying folk. You are not alone; you are a cell in the body of the Church—that is, of Christ. Through them you learn the patience that is necessary not only for the body but also for the heart and mind, for the building up of your faith.

The complete and correct prayer is one in which the words of the prayer are accepted by both thought and emotion; attentiveness is therefore needful. Do not let your thoughts wander; imprison them again and again, and always begin anew from the point where you left

---

*These prayers may be found in English in *A Manual of Eastern Orthodox Prayers* (London: S.P.C.K., 1945).

off praying. You may read from the Psalter, in the same way, especially if you do not have a prayer book. Thus you learn patience and watchfulness.

A person standing at an open window hears the sounds from outside; it is impossible not to do so. But he can give the voices his attention or not, as he himself wishes. The praying person is continually beset by a stream of inappropriate thoughts, feelings and mental impressions. To stop this tiresome stream is as impracticable as to stop the air from circulating in an open room. But one can notice them or not. This, say the saints, one learns only through practice.

When you pray, you yourself must be silent. You do not pray to have your own earthbound desires fulfilled, but you pray: Thy will be done. It is not fitting to wish to use God as an errand boy. You yourself must be silent; let the prayer speak.

Your prayer must have four constituent parts, says Basil the Great: adoration, thanksgiving, confession of sin and petition for salvation.

Do not be concerned with or pray for any private matters, but *seek ye first the kingdom of*

*God and his righteousness, and all these things shall
be added unto you* (Matthew 6:33).

He who cannot make his will and hence his
prayer coincide with God's will, will meet ob-
stacles in his undertakings and constantly fall
into the enemy's ambush. He becomes discon-
tented or angry, unhappy, perplexed or impatient or troubled; and in such a state of mind no
one can remain in prayer.

A prayer offered while one has any cause to
reproach a fellow man is an impure prayer.
There is only one whom the praying person
may and must reproach, and that is himself.
Without self-reproach, your prayer is as worthless as it is while you are reproaching someone
else in your heart. Perhaps you ask: How can
one learn this? The answer is: One learns it
through prayer.

Do not fear the drought within you. The life-
giving rain comes from above, not from your
own hard soil below, which brings forth only
thorns and thistles (Genesis 3:18). Do not wait,
therefore, for any "state," for ecstasy or rapture
or other desire-laden experiences. Prayer is not
for the sake of enjoyment. *Be afflicted and mourn
and weep* (James 4:9), remember your mortal-
ity, and call upon the Lord for mercy. The rest
depends on Him.

Chapter Eighteen

ON PRAYER

PRAYER does not stop when morning devotions are over. Now it is a matter of maintaining prayer the whole day through, no matter what the day's complications. Bishop Theophan advises the beginner to choose a suitable short sentence of prayer from the Psalter, for example, *O Lord, make haste to help me,* or *Create in me a clean heart, O God,* or *Blessed art Thou, O Lord,* or some other. The Psalter offers a wide choice of such more or less brief prayers. Later, as the day goes on, one may keep this prayer in mind and repeat it as often as possible, mentally or in a whisper or, better still, aloud as soon as one is alone and unheard. In a bus or a lift, at work and during meals, constantly, as soon as one has opportunity, one recaptures the prayer and fixes all his attention on the content of the words. Thus the day is filled until the evening reading from the prayer book in the quiet moments before going to bed.

This practice is also suitable for those who do not enjoy the privacy that is necessary for regular evening and morning devotions, for it can be carried out wherever and whenever one wishes. Inner solitude is in such cases a substitute for the external solitude that is lacking.

Frequent repetition is important: with frequent wing-beats a bird soars up over the clouds; the swimmer must repeat his strokes countless times before he reaches the desired shore. But if the bird ceases to fly, it must be content to dwell among the mists of earth. And close beneath the swimmer lurk dark and threatening depths.

Pray in this way hour after hour, day after day, without growing weary. But pray simply, not with pathos nor plodding nor with all manner of questions: do not be anxious for tomorrow (Matthew 6:34). When the time comes, you will get your answer.

Abraham set forth without wondering curiously: What does the land look like, that Thou wilt show me? What is awaiting me there? He simply set out and *departed as the Lord had spoken unto him* (Genesis 12:4). Do likewise. Abraham took all his possessions with him, and in that respect you ought to do as he did. Take everything you have, your whole being with you on your wandering; leave nothing behind that could bind your affection to the land where many gods are worshipped, the land you have left.

It took Noah a hundred years to build his Ark; log upon log he dragged to the construction. Do as he did; drag log upon log to your construction, patiently, in silence, day after day, and do not inquire about your surroundings. Remember that Noah was the only one in the whole world who *walked with God* (Genesis 6:9), that is, in prayer. Imagine the crowding, the darkness, the stench, that he had to live in until he could step out into the pure air and build an altar to the Lord. The air and the altar you will find within you, explains St. John Chrysostom, but only after you have willingly gone through the same narrow gate as Noah.

In this manner do all that the Lord commands you to do (Genesis 6:22), and build *with all prayer and supplication* (Ephesians 6:18) the bridge that takes you away from your carnal self and its divided interests to the wholeness of the Spirit. With the coming of the Only One into your heart, plurality vanishes, says Basil the Great. Your days become whole, secured by Him who holds the whole world in His hand.

Chapter Nineteen

ON THE BODILY AND MENTAL ACCOMPA-NIMENTS OF PRAYER

I T is important, while practising prayer in this way, not to give the body free rein. A prayer in which the body is not distressed and the heart grieved is like an incompletely developed fetus, says St. Isaac the Syrian, for such a prayer has no soul. And it carries within it the seed of self-sufficiency and pride that makes the heart consider itself not only among the called but even among the chosen few (Matthew 22:14).

Beware of this kind of prayer; it is the root of many errors. For if the heart is bound to the carnal, your treasure also remains in the carnal, while you think, even so, that you hold heaven in your carnal embrace. Your joy becomes impure and expresses itself in lack of control and the urge to prattle and instruct and convert others without being appointed by the Church to the calling of teacher. You interpret Scripture according to your carnal mind and cannot bear to be contradicted, and engage in hot arguments for the sake of your opinion, all because you have neglected to discipline your body and thereby humble your heart.

True joy is quiet and constant, wherefore the apostle urges us to *rejoice evermore* (I Thessalonians 5:16). It proceeds from a heart that weeps over the world's (and its own) turning from the Light; true joy is to be found in grief. For it is said: *Blessed are they that mourn* (Matthew 5:4) and *Blessed are ye that weep now* with your carnal self *for ye shall laugh* with your spiritual (Luke 6:21). True joy is the joy of consolation, the joy that wells up in the knowledge of one's own weakness and the Lord's mercy, and that does not need the bared teeth of laughter to express itself.

Think also of this: the person who is bound to earthly things may rejoice but may also be upset or disturbed or grieved over earthly things: his mind is exposed to continual changes. But the joy of your master (Matthew 25:21) is enduring, for God is unchangeable.

Thus control your tongue at the same time as you discipline your body with fasting and strictness. Talkativeness is a great enemy of prayer. A spate of fluttering words stands in the way of the words of prayer. This is the reason that we shall render account for every careless word we utter (Matthew 12:36). One does not bring the dust of the road into a room that one wishes to keep clean; thus keep your heart free from gossip and chatter about the events of the day that is past.

The tongue is a fire, and consider *how great a matter a little fire kindleth* (James 3:5–6). But if one gives a blaze no air, it dies out: if you do not give air to your passions they are gradually quenched. If you are kindled to anger, be silent and do not let it be noticed outwardly. Only the Lord may hear your confession. Thus you extinguish the burning brand at the beginning. If you are disturbed over the mistakes of another, follow the example of Shem and Japheth: cover them with the mantle of silence (Genesis 9:23); thus you quench your desire to judge before it bursts into flame. Silence can be filled with watchful prayer as a bowl holds water.

But it is not only the tongue that the person who practises the art of watchfulness must control. He must look to himself (Galatians 6:1) in every detail, and his care must extend to the depths of his being. Deep within he finds immeasurable store-rooms, where memories and thoughts and fantasies stir about and must be restrained. Do not stir up a memory that will cover your prayer with mud, do not root around in the soil of your old sins. Do not be like the dog that *returneth to his vomit* (Proverbs 26:11). Do not let your memory linger on private matters that can reawaken your desire or set your imagination going. The devil's favourite wrestling-place is precisely our imagination; through it he draws us to further intercourse with him, to consent and action. In your thought-world he sows doubt and worry, attempts at logical reasoning and proof, fruitless questions and self-found answers. Meet all such things with the words of the Psalm: *Away from me ye wicked* (Psalm 119:115).

Chapter Twenty

ON FASTING

ASTING, neither above nor below your ability, will help you in your vigil. One should not ponder divine matters on a full stomach, say the ascetics. For the well-fed, even the most superficial secrets of the Trinity lie hidden. Christ Himself set the example with His long fast; when He drove out the devil He had fasted for forty days. Are we better than He? *Behold, angels came and ministered unto him* (Matthew 4:11). They are waiting to minister to you, too.

Fasting tempers loquacity, says St. John Climacus. It is an outlet for compassion and a guard upon obedience; it destroys evil thoughts and roots out the insensibility of the heart. Fasting is a gate to paradise: when the stomach is constricted, the heart is humbled. He who fasts prays with a sober mind, but the mind of the intemperate person is filled with impure fancies and thoughts.

Fasting is an expression of love and devotion, in which one sacrifices earthly satisfaction to attain the heavenly. Altogether too much of one's thoughts are taken up with care for sustenance and the enticements of the palate; one wishes to be free from them. Thus fasting is a step on the road of emancipation and an indispensable support in the struggle against selfish desires. Together with prayer, fasting is one of humanity's greatest gifts, carefully cherished by those who once have participated in it.

During fasting, thankfulness grows toward him who has given humanity the possibility of fasting. Fasting opens the entrance to a territory that you have scarcely glimpsed: the expressions of life and all the events around you and within you get a new illumination, the hastening hours a new, wide-eyed and rich purpose. The vigil of groping thought is replaced by a vigil of clarity; troublesome searching is changed to quiet acceptance in gratitude and humility. Seemingly large, perplexing problems open their centres like the ripe calyces of flowers: with prayer, fasting and vigil in union, we may knock on the door we wish to see opened.

Here we find the reason that fasting is often used as a measuring-stick by the holy Fathers: he who fasts much is he who loves much, and he who has loved much is forgiven much (Luke 7:47). He who fasts much also receives much.

The holy Fathers recommend "moderate" fasting: one ought not to allow the body to be weakened too much, for then the soul, too, is harmed. Nor ought one to undertake fasting too suddenly: everything demands practice, and each one should look to his own nature and occupation. To choose among different kinds of food is to be condemned: all food is God-given, but it is advisable to avoid such kinds as add to the body's weight and appetite: strong spices, meat, spirituous drinks and such foods as are solely for the palate's enjoyment. For the rest, one may eat what is cheap and most easily available, they say. But by "moderate" they mean one meal a day, and that one light enough not to fill the stomach to satiety.

Chapter Twenty-One

ON THE AVOIDANCE
OF EXTRAVAGANCE

I T is a known fact that a person who practises the piano too zealously gets cramp in his hands, and a too diligent writer exposes himself to writer's cramp. Dejected and downcast, the musician or author, just now so full of hope, must break off his work; in idleness he is exposed to many evil influences.

From this example you should take warning. Fasting, obedience, self-discipline, watchfulness, prayer all make up the constituent parts necessary for practice, and only *practice*. And any practice should be always undertaken genuinely, quietly taking into account one's own resources of strength (Luke 14:28–32), and without exaggeration at any point. *Be ye therefore sober and watch unto prayer,* advises the holy apostle Peter, and through him the Lord (I Peter 4:7).

Drunkenness does not always originate in alcohol and other means of inebriation. Just as dangerous is the drunkenness that springs from all too great self-trust and the eagerness that ensues. With an abandoned zeal that expresses itself in exaggerations and extravagances, it sows its sacrifice on the soil of practice. The crop that shoots up out of this is unsound: it bears such fruit as overstrain, intolerance and self-righteousness. No, here it is a matter of not turning *aside to the right hand or to the left* (Deuteronomy 5:32) and never having the slightest confidence in one's own strength.

If we do not find within us rich fruits of love, peace, joy, moderation, humility, simplicity, uprightness, faith and patience, all our work is in vain, points out St. Macarius of Egypt. The work is carried on for the sake of the harvest, but the harvest is the Lord's.

Therefore, keep watch over yourself and be deliberate. If you notice that you are becoming irritable and intolerant, lighten your load a little. If you have the desire to look askance at others, to reproach or instruct or make remarks, you are on the wrong road: he who denies himself, has nothing with which to reproach others. If you think you are becoming "disturbed" by people or by external circumstances, you have not understood your work aright: everything that at first glance appears disturbing is really given as an opportunity for practice in tolerance, patience and obedience. The humble man cannot be disturbed, he can only disturb. Therefore keep yourself under, hide yourself. Go into your room and shut the door (Matthew 6:6), even when of necessity you find yourself in a large and noisy company. But if this sometimes becomes too hard to bear, go out anywhere where you can be alone, and cry out from your whole soul for help from the Lord, and He will hear you.

Think of yourself always as like a wheel, advises Ambrose: the more lightly the wheel touches the earth, the more easily it rolls forward. Do not think of or speak of or concern yourself with earthly matters more than is necessary. Remember, too, that a wheel that is completely in the air cannot roll.

Chapter Twenty-Two

ON THE USE OF
MATERIAL THINGS

WE are made up of soul *and* body; the two cannot be separated in our conduct. Let the physical therefore come to your aid: Christ knew our weakness and for our sake used words and gestures, spittle and earth as media. For our sake He let His power flow from the fringe of His garment (Matthew 9:20; 14:36), from the handkerchiefs or aprons that were carried away from the apostle Paul's body (Acts 19:12), yes, from the shadow of the apostle Peter (Acts 5:15).

Therefore use all that is of earth as a staff of remembrance on your troublesome wandering along the narrow way. May the whiteness of the snow and the blue of the heavens, the jewelled eye of the fly and the scorching of the

flame, and all of creation that meets your
senses, remind you of your Creator; but make
use especially of what the Church offers you to
help you *yield your members servants to righteousness unto holiness* (Romans 6:19). First of all, the
Lord's Holy Communion. But likewise the
other mysteries, or sacraments, and the holy
Scriptures. And the Church offers you also the
holy icons* of the Mother of God, the angels
and the saints; and prayer before them, and
candles and incense, holy water and the gleam of
gold, and singing. Receive all this with gratitude
and use it all for your upbuilding and
encouragement, improvement and benefit as
you travel further.

Give free outlet to your love for the generous
Lord of love, kiss the Cross and the icons,
adorn them with flowers; if only evil be
crushed with silence, the good will be allowed
to breathe freely. If what is given in love is received with love, the scope of love is increased

---

*Icons are representations of sacred persons or events painted
upon panels of wood of varying sizes. To the practising Orthodox,
however, the icon, which plays a large part in his devotional life,
is more than a mere picture. Worthily used, it is a means of contact
with the original of the picture, and a sort of window which opens
upon the unseen world.

and enlarged, and this is the aim of your work. The greater the river, the wider the delta.

Use your own body, too, as an aid in the struggle. Trim it down and make it independent of earthly whims. Let it share your trouble: you wish to learn humility, so let the body also be humble and bow to the ground. Fall on your knees with your face to the earth as often as you can in privacy, but get up at once, for after a fall follows restoration in Christ.

Make the sign of the Cross assiduously: it is a wordless prayer. In a brief moment, independent of sluggish words, it gives expression to your will to share Christ's life and crucify your flesh, and willingly, without grumbling, to receive all that the Holy Trinity sends. Moreover, the sign of the Cross is a weapon against evil spirits: use this weapon often and with reflection.

A house is never built until the scaffolding is raised. Only the strong man has no need of outward support. But are you strong? Are you not the weakest among the weak? Are you not a child?

Chapter Twenty-Three

ON TIMES OF
DARKNESS

THE weather shifts from cloudy to clear and then back to rain: thus it is with human nature. One must always expect clouds to hide the sun sometimes. Even the saints have had their dark hours, days and weeks. They say then that "God has left them" in order that they may know truly how utterly wretched they are of themselves, without His support. These times of darkness, when all seems meaningless, ridiculous and vain, when one is beset by doubt and temptations, are inevitable. But even these times can be harvested for good.

The dark days can best be conquered by following the example of St. Mary of Egypt. For forty-eight years she dwelt in the desert beyond Jordan, and when temptations befell her and memories of her former sinful life in Alexandria beckoned her to leave her voluntary sojourn in the desert, she lay on the ground, cried to God for help and did not get up until her heart was humbled. The first years were hard; she sometimes had to lie this way for many days; but after seventeen years came the time of rest.

On such days stay quiet. Do not be persuaded to go out into social life or entertainment. Do not pity yourself, seek comfort in nothing but your cry to the Lord: *Haste thee, O God, to deliver me! Make haste to help me, O Lord* (Psalm 70:1)! *I am so fast in prison that I cannot get forth* (Psalm 88:8), and other such appeals. You cannot expect real help from any other source. For the sake of chance relief do not throw away all your winnings. Pull the covers over your head: now your patience and steadfastness are being tried. If you endure the trial, thank God who gave you the strength. If you do not, rise up promptly, pray for mercy and think: I got what I deserved! For the fall itself was your punishment. You had relied too much on yourself, and now you see what it led to. You have had an experience; do not forget to give thanks.

Chapter Twenty-Four

ON AN INTERPRETATION OF ZACCHAEUS

LIKE Zacchaeus you have now climbed up into a tree to see the Lord (Luke 19). You have done so not only by your power of thought or in a mystical, mental way. You are a human being and you have a body: therefore like Zacchaeus you have made use of your strength of limb and of earthly things to climb up from the ground. And if you have done so with understanding and quiet calculation, in consciousness of your own body's weight and limitations, but without fear or foolishness or side glances, you have also been fortunate enough to raise yourself so high that you can catch, over the milling mob of mankind, that is, your earthly impulses, a glimpse of Him you sought.

You observe that as you have begun to get a clearer sense of your own darkness, you are no longer drawn so strongly as before to entertainment and social life, and you have received, as it were, a little glimpse of your inner humanity as it really is. You think, perhaps, that up to now your heart has most resembled a nutshell of a boat rocking about without destination or helmsman; now the voyage has taken on goal and meaning, and happily so. None the less you are the same little nutshell of a boat on the wide sea; if you have voyaged aright you now see for the first time clearly *how* weak and small the boat is.

If only we show our good intention, the Lord is always Himself our Guide, says Archbishop Theophylact from Bulgaria. Jesus tells Zacchaeus: *Make haste and come down;* (that is, humble yourself), *for today I must abide at thy house* (Luke 19:5). *House* here can be understood as the heart. Truly, says the Lord, you have climbed up into a tree and conquered a part of your earthly desires because you wanted to see me, that is: you wanted to be able to perceive me when I passed that way in your heart. But make haste now to humble yourself lest you sit there thinking you are better than others, for it is in the heart of the humble that I must dwell. *And he made haste and came down and received him joyfully* (verse 6).

Zacchaeus, chief of the publicans, now received Christ, and the first thing he did was to give away all that he possessed. For half of his goods he gave straightway to the poor, and the remainder surely was quickly expended to repay fourfold those from whom he had demanded too much. *He also is a son of Abraham* (verse 9): he has heard the Lord's voice and has gone from his country and from his father's house (Genesis 12:1), where selfishness and passions ruled.

Zacchaeus knew that the heart which receives Christ must empty itself of everything else: it must offer all it has of illegitimately acquired riches: *the lust of the flesh and the lust of the eyes and the pride of life* (I John 2:16). He understood that he who is rich here is poor there, for to be physically rich is the same as being spiritually poor, explains John Chrysostom: for if the rich man were not so poor, he would never be so rich.

As impossible as to unite health and sickness is to reconcile love and wealth, Isaac the Syrian points out, for he who loves his fellow men gives away unconditionally all that he possesses: such is the nature of love. But without love there is no possibility of entering the kingdom of God. This Zacchaeus observed also.

But the less you possess, the simpler is your mode of life. All excess has been thrown away, and the heart gathers itself together at its core. Little by little it tries to get into the kernel, where the stairs to heaven are to be found.

Then prayer, too, becomes simpler. Prayers gather around the centre and enter it. There in the depths is seen the only prayer that is needful: the prayer for mercy.

For what can a sinner, and *the chief* among them (I Timothy 1:15) desire other than that the Lord might have mercy on him? Has he anything to give? Does he have strength of his own, a will of his own, any composure of his own? Can he undertake anything by himself? Does he know anything? Does he understand, does he perceive anything, that he, who owns nothing, can call his own?

He owns nothing: for sin is nothingness, that which does not exist. Sin is emptiness, darkness, denial. There the sinner rests, in that nothingness.

As such he sees himself, and the less he himself possesses, the richer he is: for the emptied room within him is filled not with perishable goods, but with the fullness of eternal life, its light and its affirmation—love and mercy. It is the Lord who dwells as guest in his house.

But how can he, this sinner, merit the Lord's arrival? How can he ever imagine that the Lord will look upon him in his darkness? However he tries to cleanse himself, however he struggles and works, however he follows the commandment of the Gospel and watches and fasts and in every way endeavours to deny himself for the Lord's sake, he sees himself even so fall back into ill humour and quarrelsomeness, lovelessness and laziness, impatience and ingratitude and all imaginable vices. How can he ever expect the Lord to come into such a room?

Therefore he prays: Lord, have mercy. Have mercy on me, a sinner. For truly I have tried to do *what it was my duty* to do to serve Thee: I have *ploughed* the field of my heart that Thou gavest me to tend, and I have *fed the cattle* there (Luke 17:7–10), but I am only Thy humble servant and without Thee I can do nothing. So have mercy on me and fill me with Thy grace.

Through work he increases his faith (Luke 17:5), through prayer he gets strength to work.

Thus work and prayer live closely together, until they flow together and become one. His work becomes to pray, and his prayer is his work. This is what the saints call spiritual activity, the prayer of the heart, or the Jesus Prayer.

Chapter Twenty-Five

ON THE JESUS PRAYER*

THE saintly Abbot Isaiah, the Egyptian hermit, says of the Jesus Prayer that it is a mirror for the mind and a lantern for the conscience. Someone has also likened it to a constantly sounding, quiet voice in a house: all thieves that sneak in take hasty flight when they hear that someone is awake there. The house is the heart, the thieves, the evil impulses. Prayer is the voice of the one who keeps watch. But

---

*"Lord Jesus Christ, Son of God, have mercy on me," to which the words "a sinner" are sometimes added, is a form of devotion of great antiquity in Eastern Christendom. The use of it is widespread among members of the Orthodox Church. More may be read about it in "La méthode de l'oraison hésychaste" by J. Hausherr in *Orientalia Christiana* 9 (2), 1927. What the Jesus Prayer meant to a simple Russian pilgrim in the nineteenth century may be seen in much more popular form in *The Way of a Pilgrim,* translated by R. M. French (London: S.P.C.K., new edition illustrated, 1954).

the one who keeps watch is no longer I, but Christ.

Spiritual activity embodies Christ in our soul. This involves continual remembrance of the Lord: you hide Him within, in your soul, your heart, your consciousness. *I sleep, but my heart waketh* (Song of Solomon 5:2): I myself sleep, withdraw, but the heart stays steadfast in prayer, that is, in eternal life, in the kingdom of Heaven, in Christ. The tree-roots of my being stand fast in their source.

The means of attaining this is the prayer: *Lord Jesus Christ, Son of God, have mercy on me, a sinner.* Repeat it aloud, or only in thought, slowly, lingeringly, but with attention, and from a heart freed as much as possible from all that is inappropriate to it. Not only worldly interests are inappropriate, but also such things as every kind of expectation or thought of answer, or inner visions, testings, all kinds of romantic dreams, curious questions and imaginings. Simplicity is as inescapable a condition as humility, abstemiousness of body and soul, and in general everything that pertains to the invisible warfare.

Especially should the beginner beware of everything that has the slightest tendency to mysticism. The Jesus Prayer is an activity, a practical work and a means by which you enable yourself to receive and use the power called God's grace—constantly present, however hidden, within the baptized person—in order that it may bear fruit. Prayer fructifies this power in our soul; it has no other purpose. It is a hammer that crushes a shell: a hammer is hard and its stroke hurts. Abandon every thought of pleasantness, rapture, heavenly voices: there is only one way to the kingdom of God, and that is the way of the Cross. And to hang crucified on a tree is horrible torment. Expect nothing else.

You have crucified your body by nailing it fast with a simple and uniform manner of life under strict self-discipline. Your thought-life and imagination ought to be as strictly controlled. Nail them fast with the words of prayer and Holy Scripture, with the reading of Psalms and the works of the holy Fathers, where these things are commanded. Do not permit your imagination to fly about at will. What men call "the flight of thought" is usually an aimless fluttering in the world of illusions. As soon as your thoughts are not occupied in your work's behalf, let them turn again to prayer.

See to it that both imagination and thought

are as obedient to you as a well-trained dog. You do not allow it to run around and yap and rummage in garbage pails and bathe in the gutter. Likewise you ought always to be able to call back your thoughts and imagination, and you must do so untold times every passing minute. If you do not do so, you are like a horse driven now by one rider and now by another, says St. Anthony, until, worn out and lathered, it collapses.

If you hammer a nutshell too hard, you may crush the kernel as well. Lay on with caution. Do not pass over suddenly to the Jesus Prayer. Hold back to begin with, and even afterward, use your other prayer practices as well. Do not be overanxious. And do not suppose that you can pay proper attention to a single *Lord, have mercy*. Your prayer is bound to be divided and scattered: you are, indeed, human. Only *in heaven the angels do always behold the face of my Father which is in heaven* (Matthew 18:10): you, on the contrary, have an earthly body with its own cravings. Do not shriek to high heaven in amazement if at the beginning you completely forget your prayer practice for many hours at a time, perhaps for a whole day or longer. Take it naturally and simply: you are an inexperienced sailor who has been so anxiously occupied with other things that he forgot to keep watch on the breezes. Thus, expect nothing of yourself. But do not demand anything of others, either.

Concentration is one thing, distraction another. Prayer will make your thought vital and clear: then it is right. The praying person sees everything around him, notices and observes everything, but the right doing of this comes through prayer, which sheds on all things its piercingly clear light.

The spirit works in the realm of purity within us. As long as we keep extending this realm of independence of heart, our spiritual humanity will continue to grow.

Prayer will call forth an inner calm, a peaceful relaxation in grief, love, gratitude, humility. If you are, on the contrary, tense and stirred up, in high spirits or in deep despair, if you feel contrition or bitterness or an exaggerated will to action, if you are thrown into ecstatic experiences or a drunkenness of the senses, such as you enjoy when listening to music, if you feel a supreme enjoyment or satisfaction so that you are "content with yourself and the whole world," you are on the wrong road. You have built altogether too much on yourself. Sound your retreat and go back to that self-reproach that must always be the starting-point for every true prayer.

The angel of light always brings peace, the peace that the demons of the dark wish at all costs to disturb. By this, say the holy Fathers, one can recognize the evil powers and separate them from the good.

Chapter Twenty-Six

ON THE PEARL
OF GREAT PRICE

STRIPPED of all knowledge, lacking in every good thought or deed, without memory from the past or wish for the future, as useless as a worn-out rag, unfeeling as a stone in the path, corroded as a worm-eaten mushroom in the woods, mortal as a fish on the shore and grieved to tears over this wretched plight of yours, thus you will stand in prayer before the Almighty, your Judge and Creator and Father, your Saviour and Master, the Spirit of Truth and Giver of Life; and like the Prodigal Son you will stammer out of the depths of your impotency: *Father, I have sinned against heaven and in thy sight, and am no more worthy to be called thy son* (Luke 15:21). Lord Jesus Christ, Son of God, have mercy on me, a sinner.

You know your impotence and let yourself lie like a grain of dust before the Almighty, and out of your wretchedness grows love to your fellow men as those created by the Lord and aglow with Him. He in His unfathomable being takes notice of them; it is enough for you to offer everything for them.

The strange thing has now come to pass that the deeper you pressed into your own heart, the farther and higher you climbed out of yourself. The outward conditions of your life are the same: you wash dishes and care for the children, you go to work, draw your salary and pay your taxes. You do everything pertaining to your external life as a person in a society, since there is no chance of leaving it. But you have resigned yourself. You have given away one thing in order to receive another.

. . . And if I have Thee, what more do I ask on earth? Nothing, answers St. John Climacus, but ceaselessly praying, silently to cling to Thee. Some are enslaved by riches, others by honour, still others by acquiring possessions; my only desire is to cling to God.

Prayer, with all it contains of self-renunciation, has become your real life, which you keep up as though only for the sake of prayer. Walk-

ing with God (Genesis 6:9) is from now on the
only thing that has real value for you, and it
includes all heavenly and earthly events. For
him who bears Christ within himself there is
neither death nor illness or any earthly clamour;
he has already stepped into eternal life, and that
embraces everything.

Night and day the heavenly seed sprouts in
your heart and grows, you know not how. The
earth produces of itself, your heart's soil, first
the blade, then the ear, then the full grain in the
ear (Mark 4:27–8).

The saints speak of something they call the
inextinguishable light. It is a light not of the eye
but of the heart that never ceases to walk in
purity and clearness. It swiftly leaves the darkness behind, and constantly strives towards the
day's height. Its constant quality is to be continually purified. This is the light of eternity
that can never go out, and that shines through
the veil of time and matter. But the saints never
say that this light is given to them, but that it is
given only to those who have purified their
hearts in love for the Lord, on the narrow way
which they have freely chosen.

The narrow way has no end: its quality is
eternity. There every moment is a moment of

beginning—the present includes the future: the day of judgment; the present includes the past: creation; for Christ is timelessly present everywhere, both in hell and in heaven. With the coming of the One, plurality disappears, even in time and space. Everything happens simultaneously, now and here and everywhere, in the depths of your heart. There you meet what you sought: the depth and height and breadth of the Cross: the Saviour and salvation.

Therefore, if you wish to save your soul and win eternal life, arise moment by moment from your dullness, bless yourself with the sign of the Cross and say: Let me, Lord, make a good beginning, in the name of the Father and of the Son and of the Holy Ghost. Amen.

LIST OF THE FATHERS
AND AUTHORS
MENTIONED IN
THIS BOOK

The Elder AMBROSE (1812–1851). A teacher and priest-monk, and one of the most renowned elders in the monastery of Optina in the Kaluga Province of Russia. Thousands of people resorted to him as spiritual adviser, among them Dostoyevsky and Tolstoy. His letters and speeches were published in several editions (in Russian) after his death.

ANDREW of Crete. A native of Damascus, he became Archbishop of Crete (685–711). He is known especially as the author of the Great Canon, which is sung on the Thursday before Palm Sunday. A detail of interest to Anglicans is that this hymn-writer was the author of the original "Christian, dost thou see them?"

ANTHONY the Great was one of the earliest and the best known of the Desert Fathers. He was perhaps the first to gather other hermits round him in the seclusion of the Egyptian Desert. He died about A.D. 350 at a great age and his life was written by his friend, St. Athanasius.

BASIL the Great. Bishop of Caesarea in Cappadocia in the fourth century. He was one of the three great Cappadocian Fathers, the other two being St. Gregory of Nyssa (his brother) and St. Gregory of Nazianzus. He drew up the Rule which has since been followed by monks and nuns of the Eastern Orthodox Church, and he gave his name to the liturgy of St. Basil which is used in that Church on a few days in the year.

DOROTHEUS. An ascetical writer of the seventh century, and abbot of a monastery. He wrote a series of Instructions on the ascetic life.

EPHRAEM, the Syrian. A learned commentator and a voluminous writer on theological subjects, largely in verse. He lived in great austerity at Edessa, where he died in A.D. 373.

HESYCHIUS of Jerusalem. A monk who was made priest in the year 412. He was a biblical commentator and also wrote on Church history.

ISAAC of Syria. A sixth-century ascetic who for a short while was Bishop of Nineveh. But he retired to a monastery near Rabban Shapur, where he wrote on the ascetic life.

The Abbot ISAIAH. A hermit in the Egyptian Desert during the latter half of the fourth century.

JOHN CHRYSOSTOM. A man of great holiness and ascetic life. Born in 347, he was made deacon in 381 and priest in 386. He was an eloquent preacher (Chrysostom means "golden-mouthed"). Much against his will he was made Patriarch of Constantinople in 398. He won the love of the people, but the hostility of the Empress Eudoxia and the enmity of the Patriarch of Alexandria. He was sent into exile under such conditions that he soon died. The liturgy in general use in the Orthodox Church bears his name.

JOHN CLIMACUS. Author of the famous *Ladder of Paradise*. For some forty years he lived as an anchorite in a cave at the foot of Mt. Sinai. Then he became Abbot of Sinai. The *Ladder* is a treatise of thirty chapters on the monastic and ascetic life. He lived in the seventh century.

MACARIUS of Egypt; called the Great (300–390). A monk of the Egyptian Desert who became a priest in 340.

NICETAS STETHATOS. A pupil of Simeon the New Theologian in the eleventh century. He published a treatise against Rome during the quarrel between Leo IX and the Patriarch of Constantinople, Cerularius. Later he withdrew it under pressure from the Emperor.

THEOPHAN (1815–1894), Bishop of Vladimir in Russia. He was a well-known writer and spiritual adviser, but spent the last twenty-one years of his life in complete seclusion in a monastery. He was the compiler of the Russian version of the Philokalia.

THEOPHYLACT. Archbishop of Ochrida on the lake of that name in Yugoslavia, and called the Bulgarian, who died about 1107. He was much revered for his exegesis of the Gospels.

A NOTE ON THE PHILOKALIA

MOST of the Fathers referred to in this book are represented in the Philokalia, which is a collection of extracts from the works of Eastern Christian Fathers extending roughly over the thousand years which end with the fourteenth century. The original compilation was made in Greek and first published in Venice in 1782. The celebrated Paissy Velitchkovsky translated it into Church Slavonic twelve years later and thereby exercised considerable influence on the religious life of Russia. In the following century Bishop Theophan made a Russian version of the Philokalia. The title of the Slavonic and Russian versions is Dobrotolyubie. Some passages from the Philokalia, notably those treating of Prayer of the Heart and the Jesus Prayer, have been translated into English from the Russian version by E. Kadlouboysky and C. E. H. Palmer and published by Faber & Faber in 1951 under the title *Writings from the Philokalia on Prayer of the Heart*.

The following are the names of several simple and easily obtained books in English which will be of interest to readers of *Way of the Ascetics:*

Orthodox Spirituality, by a Monk of the Eastern Church (London: S.P.C.K., 1945). Contains a useful Bibliographical Note and List of Books.

The Way of a Pilgrim and *The Pilgrim Continues His Way*. Translated from the anonymous Russian by R. M. French. New Edition in one volume, illustrated (London: S.P.C.K., 1954).

A Manual of Eastern Orthodox Prayers (London: S.P.C.K., 1945).

INDEX